Bringing God's Seasons Inside

Fall/Winter Bulletin Board Designs

Written by Lisa Hahn and Wendy Nimtz * *Illustrated by Carolyn Braun*

Contents

To my husband, Mark,
for your constant encouragement—Romans 12:10–11
W.N.

To my blessings: Noah, Anna, and Nathanael — it's your turn now

And to my husband, Kevin — Romans 15:5–6
L.H.

Scripture quotations taken from the HOLY BIBLE, NEW INTERNATIONAL VERSION®. NIV®. Copyright © 1973, 1978, 1984 by International Bible Society. Used by permission of Zondervan Publishing House. All rights reserved.

Copyright © 1999 Concordia Publishing House

3558 S. Jefferson Avenue, St. Louis, MO 63118-3968

Manufactured in the United States of America

1 2 3 4 5 6 7 8 9 10   08 07 06 05 04 03 02 01 00 99

A Note to Teachers

As a 🍎 teacher, you are called to teach, not spend a lot of time 👁 putting up bulletin boards. The ideas in this book are designed to help you do just that: to *teach*. Using an interactive approach, both you and the students 😊 will work together and create a learning experience. The students will have an opportunity to be actively involved individually, in pairs, or in small groups ⚛.

A bulletin board can serve two purposes. It can be a seasonal decoration ❄, pleasing the eye . . . or it can be an interactive learning tool, 😃 stimulating the mind. In this book, we attempted to share ideas 💡 that serve both purposes simultaneously.

These bulletin boards revolve around the fall and winter seasons ❄, highlighting the holidays of the ✦ Church year that are often overlooked. Every idea 💡 involves the students in some way, either individually or in groups. Many of the ideas encourage self-expression, sharing, and an appreciation for all as God's precious ✿ children. Involving the students in the creative process will save you time and give the students a sense of 😃 ownership and pride. Using an interactive approach, you and your students can work together to create an exciting ⚡ learning experience.

We hope you enjoy using this book of 💡 ideas and expanding upon it as much as we enjoyed working together 💗 to write it. We thank God 👁 for the opportunity to share these ideas with you. What a creative Creator we have!! May God bless you and your students as you learn and grow together.

😊 Lisa and Wendy

Tips for Better Bulletin Boards

Use Shortcuts

- Cut out letters freehand. Many are symmetrical and easy to cut. Don't worry about hanging them straight. Angles can be more interesting and less time-consuming.
- Choose a background color that can be reused several times. For example, red works for September, fall, Advent, and Christmas themes. Blue works for Advent, Christmas, Epiphany, and winter themes. A black background serves to highlight student work.
- Adapt these ideas for different seasons of the year. Use flowers instead of snowflakes, ladybugs instead of Christmas wreaths.
- Change the skill written on a game piece to include other skills or additional subjects.
- Use the shapes of balloons, clouds, or leaves, and write letters directly onto them.
- Copy patterns directly onto construction paper. This eliminates the step of tracing.
- Copy the patterns in this book onto overhead masters. Use an overhead projector to make the patterns larger, if needed.
- If desired, copy and enlarge the directions for child involvement. Post these directions on or near the bulletin board.

Increase Involvement

- Challenge yourself to discover ways to involve the children by creating bulletin boards with activities for them to complete.
- Use bulletin boards to initiate creative writing projects.

- Provide paper for recording results or things learned as the activity is completed. Offer extra credit points for those in related subjects.
- Always model for the class how to complete the bulletin board activity. Include directions for putting things away when finished.

Spark Interest

- Use creative borders to set off your bulletin board design. For math bulletin boards, use number lines or math tools. For community building, use children's signatures or photographs. Use real objects for borders or decoration rather than those cut out of paper. It's more attractive and will save you time.
- Use wrapping paper, paper decorated by the children, or other creative options as background paper. This will give your bulletin board depth.
- Experiment with unconventional color combinations for backgrounds and titles. (Thanks, Tracy!)
- Let your decorations extend beyond the frame of the bulletin board.
- Use a question for a title. This piques the interest of the children and invites involvement.
- Look for as many ways as possible to involve the students when creating a bulletin board. This will help make it "theirs" and save you time.

Stay Organized

- Measure and cut the pieces of background paper you think you will use for the entire school year. Roll these pieces and store so they will be ready when needed.
- If bulletin board space is limited, adapt these ideas as learning centers and store them in shoeboxes.
- Designate when individuals will have their turn to complete the bulletin board activity. This gives everyone a chance and avoids a mad dash to the board at certain times.
- Provide envelopes and plastic bags for storage of loose pieces. Replace as needed.
- To prevent tearing, use contact paper or laminate pieces that will be handled many times.
- When taking down the bulletin board, save all pieces in a large, resealable plastic bag and label accordingly for future use.
- Take pictures of the completed bulletin boards, and keep them in a photo album. (Great idea, C.J.!)

Each bulletin board design features involvement by both the children and adults.

☺ *indicates directions for child involvement.*

🍎 *indicates directions for teacher involvement.*

Who's "Back" to School?
*Getting to know each other   *Self-expression

☺ Place your head on a piece of paper and have a friend trace around the outline of your head and hair. Cut out the outline of your head. Color it to match your hair. Turn it around and draw your face.

☺ Bring in a white T-shirt (or use a paper outline of a T-shirt). Place a piece of paper or cardboard inside the shirt so your markers will not show through to the other side. On the front of the T-shirt, write and decorate your first and last name. On the back, draw a picture or write about something you like to do to serve Jesus.

🍎 Pair the heads and corresponding T-shirts. Hang them up together with the backs of the heads and T-shirts showing. Tell the children to keep their identities a secret. Choose one or two T-shirts each day, and have the children guess the identity. Turn the face and T-shirt around to reveal the name and face.

💡 **A Different Twist**

1. Use photographs instead of drawing heads.
2. Make T-shirts for other occasions. Draw your pet, a pet you wish you had, your favorite place, your favorite food or sport, your family, your favorite Bible story, etc. Play the guessing game again.

We Fit Together as One

*Working together   *Community building

Cut a 3′ × 2′ piece of poster board to resemble a puzzle. Cut it into the same number of pieces as children in your class. Give each child a piece of the puzzle.

Choose pictures from magazines that best describe you. Cut out the pictures and glue them onto your puzzle piece. Cover the entire puzzle piece with a collage of pictures.

Share your puzzle piece with the class. After everyone has had a turn, work together to fit the whole puzzle together.

Display the puzzle on the bulletin board.

WE FIT TOGETHER AS ONE

Mark   Sue

Haily   Jose

Robert   Whitney

Elizabeth   Jim

A Different Twist

1. Have the children draw or write about themselves on the puzzle piece.
2. Have each child partner with a different person in class. Have them ask questions that would help them get to know each other. What do you like to do on Saturdays? What is your favorite sport? What kind of books do you like? The children will then decorate the puzzle piece of their partner. Using the puzzle pieces, have the children introduce each other to the class.

What's Your Story?

*Community building *Writing skills *Public speaking

Write the following story on a large piece of poster board, leaving an 8" space for every blank.

My name is _____. I like to eat _____ and _____. I like to play _____. My favorite color is _____. At school I like to _____. At home I like to _____. When I am with my family, I like to _____.

Using eight 3" × 5" index cards, write or draw the following statements, each on a separate card: your name, a favorite food (two cards), a favorite play activity, your favorite color, a favorite thing to do at school, a favorite thing to do at home, and a favorite thing to do with your family.

Each day during the first month of school, choose a different child to add his or her cards to the story and read it to the class.

A Different Twist

1. Give each child a poster board story to complete. Post the stories on a bulletin board for other children to read.

3

Pile 'Em Up!

*Classifying

☺ Draw colorful leaves of any shape or size and cut them out. Put the paper leaves in a basket near the bulletin board.

🍎 Make rakes and label them as follows: Jagged, Bumpy, Smooth, Yellow, Orange, Brown, Multicolored, Big, Medium, and Small. Add any other words that describe leaves.

🍎 Hang three rakes on the bulletin board at a time. Place a gallon-sized plastic bag beneath each rake. (This allows the leaves to be seen well.)

☺ Read the word on each rake, and categorize the leaves by placing them in the correct bags. Show your teacher when a bag is full.

🍎 Change rakes and categories every few days.

💡 A Different Twist

1. This ideas also works well with snowflakes and shovels for winter or flowers and garden tools for spring.

2. Have smaller children color a sheet of paper. Let adults cut the colored paper into leaves.

Pile 'Em up!

JAGGED

BUMPY

SMOOTH

4

What Acorn-y Story
*Creative writing   *Public speaking

🍎 Create a border by stapling real or paper oak leaves around the bulletin board.

🍎 Copy the acorn story pattern onto light brown paper (see pattern on page 52).

☺ Write a creative, funny story that could happen in the fall or at the beginning of the school year. Share your story with others in the class.

🍎 Display the stories on the bulletin board after they are read to the rest of the class.

💡 **A Different Twist**

After a few weeks, take the stories down from the bulletin board, and bind them together to make a class book everyone can enjoy reading.

Piles of Practice

*Math or spelling practice   *Working with a partner

Fashion a large, paper tree on one side of the bulletin board. Tan crinkle-ribbon can be pulled apart to make the trunk. Add twisted crinkle-ribbon for branches.

Cut out leaf shapes using fall colors (see pattern on page 53). Laminate or cover the leaves with clear contact paper to reuse. Write concepts to be reviewed (i.e. math facts, spelling words, long vowel words) on each leaf. Use pins to attach the leaves to the tree. Staple a few blank leaves at the bottom of the tree to start a pile.

Choose a partner. Use the leaves on the tree to quiz one another. When you answer correctly, add that leaf to the pile by the side of the tree. When finished, pin the leaves back onto the tree.

Piles of Practice

Which Apples Are Proper?

*Capitalization

☺ Use a variety of art media to make apples.

🍎 Fashion a paper tree on the bulletin board (see directions for previous bulletin board). Write various nouns, common and proper, on the apples. Be sure to capitalize the proper nouns. Pin the apples to the tree. Add two baskets to the bottom of the bulletin board. Label them "common" and "proper."

☺ Play this bulletin board game by removing the nouns from the tree and placing them in the correct basket.

💡 **A Different Twist**

1. Add an alphabetized list of correct answers inside each basket for self-checking.

2. Have the children do this activity with a partner. When a proper noun is found, state why it is capitalized. Baskets could even be made for specific types of proper nouns.

Name That Pumpkin!
*Classifying

☺ Be creative and make orange pumpkins with faces.

🍎 Arrange the pumpkins on the bulletin board according to various characteristics—round-nosed pumpkins, happy pumpkins, silly pumpkins, bumpy pumpkins, and smooth pumpkins. Write the title of the group on the back of a paper rectangle placed above each group. Staple an envelope under each group of pumpkins. Place blank slips of paper on or near the bulletin board.

☺ Look at each group of pumpkins. What is the same about all of the pumpkins in each group? Think of a title describing each group like bumpy pumpkins or happy pumpkins. Write your ideas for titles on blank pieces of paper, and place them in the envelopes below each group of pumpkins.

🍎 Every few days, read the titles in the envelopes. Reveal the actual title of the group. Rearrange the pumpkins according to different characteristics and play again.

Name That Pumpkin!

▲-eyed pumpkins

How Can Jesus' Light Shine through Me?

*Sharing the faith   *Creativity   *Positive reinforcement

Choose a dark background (other than orange) to cover the bulletin board. Cut letters for the title out of yellow or orange paper. Place the title at the top.

Cut pumpkin shapes out of orange paper and leaf shapes out of green paper (see pattern on page 54).

Use a scissors to carve out a happy, joyful face on your paper pumpkin. Glue yellow paper behind your pumpkin so the yellow shows through. This will make the face glow. (Younger children may simply want to glue yellow eyes, nose, and mouth shapes onto the pumpkin.)

On paper leaves, write or draw ways to share the Gospel message of Jesus with others by being a light to a dark world. These can be expressed through words or deeds.

A Different Twist

1. Catch children being good. Write the good behavior on a leaf, and add it to that child's pumpkin.
2. Have children choose a Bible verse that encourages them to share their faith, and write the verse on a leaf.

Faith Alone—Grace Alone—Scripture Alone (Reformation)

*Bible skills *Cooperative group work

Divide the board into three sections, one for each part of the title: Faith Alone, Grace Alone, and Scripture Alone. *Sola Fide*, *Sola Gratia*, and *Sola Scriptura* can also be used.

Make copies of the cross, heart, and Bible pattern, one of each per child (see pattern on page 55). Use the cross for faith alone, the heart for grace alone, and the Bible for Scripture alone.

Search God's Word for a verse about faith in Jesus Christ (faith alone), and write the verse on the cross. Look for a verse about God's free gift of grace to all believers (grace alone), and write the verse on the heart. Find a Bible verse that tells about the good news of salvation as revealed in God's Word (Scripture alone), and write the verse on the Bible.

You can work alone or in groups. Use a concordance or catechism for help. Share the verses found with the class.

Staple the crosses, hearts, and Bibles in the correct section of the bulletin board.

💡 A Different Twist

1. Have the class work in three groups, one each for faith, grace, and Scripture. Each group should find five or more verses, and write each on a note card. Mix the cards up, and place them in a large plastic bag or envelope at the bottom of the bulletin board. Have the children take turns pinning verses under the correct heading. Draw the matching symbol on the back of each note card so the activity will be self-checking.

God's Word Is Truth

✳ Reformation/Bible truths

Divide the children into four groups. Give each group a portion of the large Luther's Seal from the bulletin board (see patterns on page 56–57) and an explanation of its meaning.

- Gold: Heaven's joy never ends.
- Blue: We have the promise and hope of heaven.
- White: Angels are watching over us, rejoicing with us in heaven.
- Red: Our faith brings love, joy, and peace to our hearts.

Using a concordance, find 2–3 Bible verses that tell about your part of Luther's seal. (Or, the teacher could provide some suggestions.)

Write the verses on your part of Luther's seal. Write on the edges so the words will not be covered when the seal is put back together.

Keep the black cross at your desk. As the children work, call each one to your desk to write a sin on the cross. When you hang the seal on the bulletin board, hang the cross with the blank side showing. Talk about why the sins do not show anymore and relate the discussion to God's gift of grace through the death and resurrection of Jesus.

GOD'S WORD   IS TRUTH

Jesus Christ is the same yesterday, today and forever. Hebrews 13:8

"I will give you the crown of Life."

He will command His angels to guard you. Psalm 91

💡 A Different Twist

1. As an ongoing project, cut additional smaller shapes of the various parts of the seal. Allow the children to find additional verses; write them on the appropriate shape, and hang them around the seal.

O, Give Thanks unto the Lord

*Thankfulness   *Food pyramid/health   *Setting a table

Use brown or orange paper to create a large rectangle in the middle of the bulletin board.

On a white paper plate, draw or glue pictures of food for which you are thankful. Include each group of the food pyramid: bread, dairy, fruit and vegetable, and meat.

Staple a place mat for each child onto the rectangle as if you were setting a table. Add each child's plate and name to a place mat.

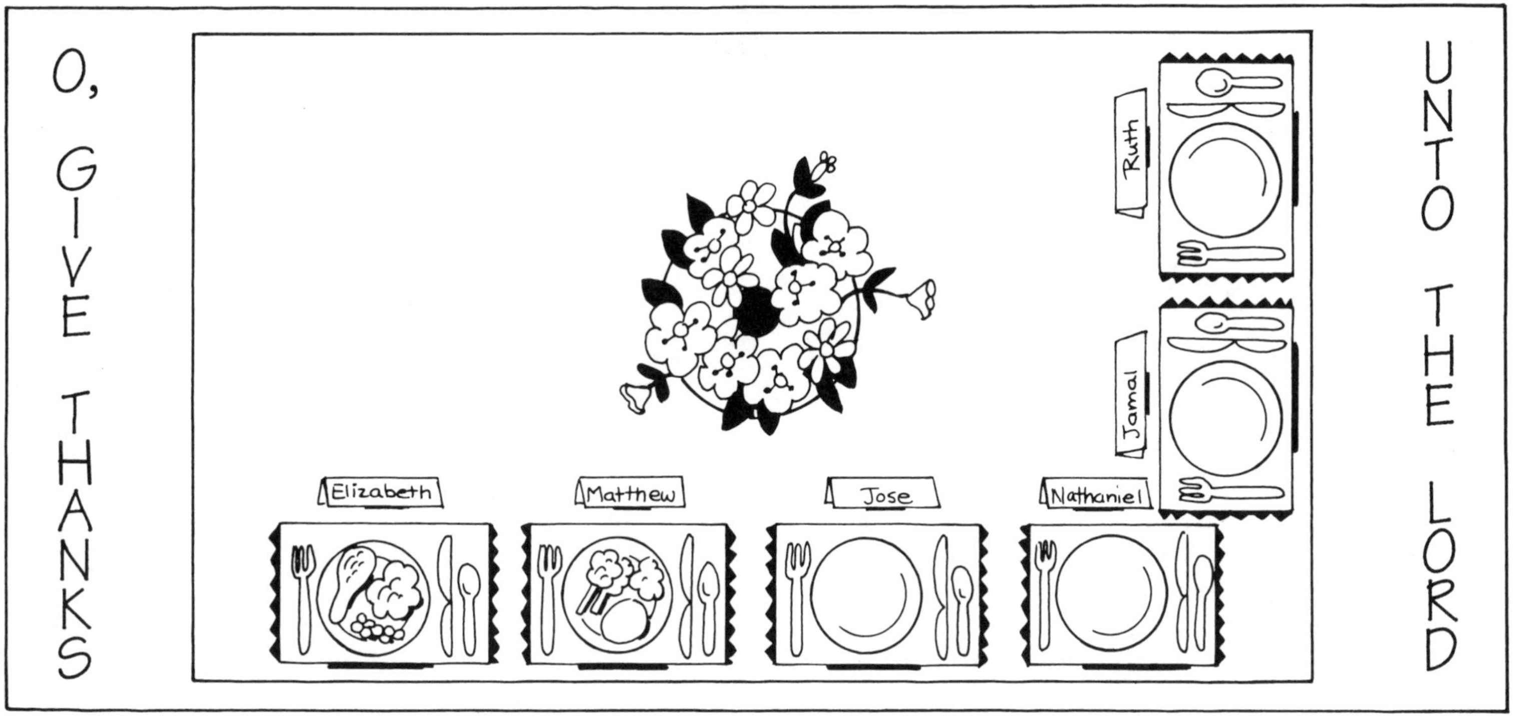

A Different Twist

1. Glue the paper plate to a place mat and add a napkin and plastic utensils to practice the skill of table setting.

Pray, Praise, and Give Thanks

*Elements of prayer   *Sharing prayers out loud

Hang a large set of folding hands in the center of the bulletin board. Place the word "Pray" above it. Staple the words "Praise" to the left and "Give Thanks" to the right of the folding hands.

Discuss how prayers of praise and thanksgiving take the focus off of us and shift it to our heavenly Father. Include Bible stories such as "The Ten Lepers" (Luke 17:11–19), "The Parable of the Pharisee and the Tax Collector" (Luke 18:9–14), and "Jesus' Teaching on Prayer" (Matthew 6:5–13 and Luke 11:1–13) as examples.

Close your hand and place it on a piece of paper. Trace around your hand two times. Cut out each handprint. On one paper hand, write a prayer that expresses praise to God. On the other, write a prayer that gives thanks to God. Add them to the bulletin board in the correct places.

Take turns using these prayers in opening or closing devotions.

13

It's Harvest Time ... Blessings Abound!

*Social studies/Categorizing

🍎 Make paper wagons and a tractor to hang on the bulletin board. Label the wagons "Grains," "Vegetables," and "Fruits."

☺ Cut out or draw pictures of foods you have eaten today. (Or, if everyone brings their lunch, use daily lunches.) Food labels could also be used.

☺ Staple your "foods" to the proper wagons on the bulletin board. If your food does not match a wagon, staple it along the bottom of the bulletin board.

Grains   Vegetables   Fruits

💡 A Different Twist

1. Use the bulletin board for a springboard for thank-You prayers before or after lunch.
2. Have the children use a fair-style blue ribbon to mark their favorite foods. Be sure to add the children's names to the blue ribbons.

14

Pumpkin Pie Math
Multiplication practice

🍎 Choose a fall color as a background, and place the title at the top.

🍎 Cut six or more 15″ circles out of brown poster board. Draw lines dividing each circle into eight sections like a pie.

🍎 In each section, write the sum, difference, product, or quotient, depending on the math skill needing practice. Example: 24, 35, 12, etc. Arrange the circles across the bottom of the bulletin board. Staple or tack each circle at the center, leaving the edges of each circle free.

🍎 Write a different math problem on eight clothespins, corresponding to the eight answers written on the sections of each circle. Example: 8 × 3, 5 × 7, 2 × 6, etc. Place the clothespins in a small plastic bag, and staple it under the pie. Do this for all six pies.

☺ Work at one pie at a time. Do the problems on each clothespin and find the answer on the pie. Clip the clothespin (problem) to the correct slice of the pie (answer).

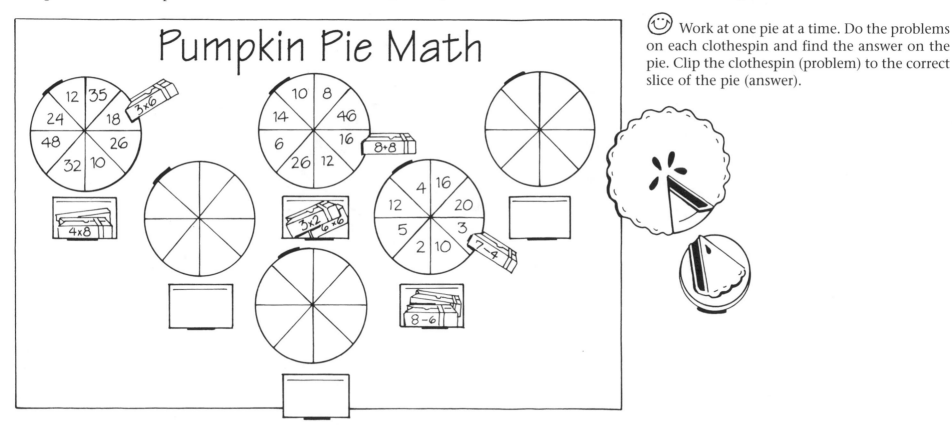

💡 A Different Twist

1. Use this activity as a learning center. The activity can be adapted to review other concepts or easily be changed to accomodate another level of difficulty.

We Thank God for Special Friends

*Thankful attitude   *Appreciation for others

🍎 Place a turkey without feathers in the center of the bulletin board. Add the title. Cut out paper feathers, using a variety of colors.

☺ Write the names of people you thank God for on one or more feathers.

🍎 Add the feathers to the turkey.

WE THANK GOD FOR SPECIAL FRIENDS

Cousin D.J.

Cousin Jessica

Grandma Ruth

Grampa Arnie

Pastor Jim

Uncle Mark

Mom, Dad

Grandma Judy

Grampa Ted

 **A Different Twist**

1. Cut out pictures of things you are thankful for and glue them to the feathers.
2. Write prayers on each feather to say at the thanksgiving meal. Have the children take the prayers home to share with their families.

The Great Icicle Challenge

*Ordering/Measuring

😊 Draw icicles on paper. The width at the top of each icicle should be the same. The length is up to you.

🍎 Laminate the icicles. Place them in order from the shortest icicle to the longest.

🍎 Make paper windows on the bulletin board. Tape facts you wish the children to practice putting in order on the icicles (i.e. books of the Bible, historical dates or events, words to be alphabetized, etc.). Each "window" could contain a different set of facts.

😊 Put each item in the proper order by hanging the icicles in order from shortest to longest.

💡 A Different Twist

1. Write the words on the laminated icicles with wipe-off crayons or markers.

2. Use this game for unscrambling a long "word for the week" or a new vocabulary word. Instruct the children to hang the icicles with the letters facing the board so the secret message isn't given away to others who have not yet played.

Who's Below the Snow?

*Science/Animals

🍎 Help children choose an animal or insect that spends the winter underground.

☺ Draw and cut out your animal and its winter home. Place it on the bulletin board.

💡 A Different Twist

1. Title the board "WHERE DO I GO WHEN GOD SENDS SNOW?" and include animals that spend the winter above ground as well.
2. Have children give oral reports to share information on different animals. Leave the homes on the board and remove the animals. Play a game of placing the animals in the correct places.

What's the Forecast?

*Geography   *Weather

🍎 Assign each of the 50 states to children or groups of children.

🍎 Obtain a large map or use an overhead projector to trace the United States.

😊 Find each state's average January temperature, average snowfall, and winter months' recreation. Put the information on a card to place near the state, or put it right on the state. Use illustrations or magazine pictures.

💡 **A Different Twist**

1. Divide the country into regions rather than doing each individual state.
2. Have the children put a pin with their name on the state in which they would like to live during the winter.

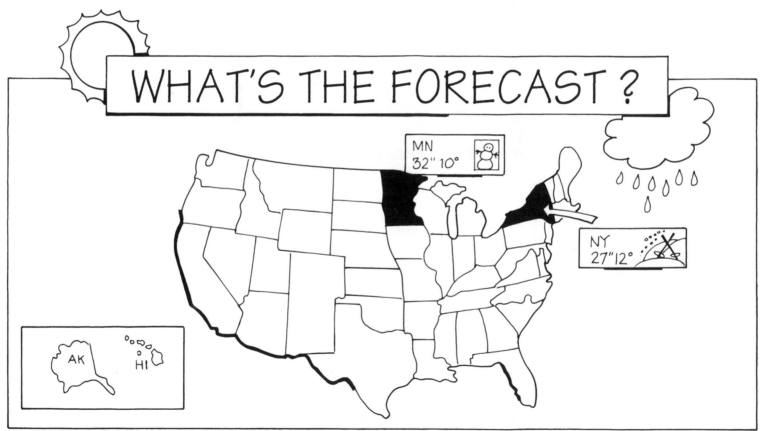

WHAT'S THE FORECAST ?

MN
32" 10°

NY
27"12°

AK   HI

We Are God's Unique Creation

*Building self-esteem   *Fine motor skills

🍎 Use a dark color for the background.

😊 Cut a snowflake shape out of a doily or white paper. Glue the snowflake onto light blue paper and trim the edges.

🍎 As children are cutting out snowflakes, connect the idea of a snowflake's uniqueness and our uniqueness as God's children.

😊 Have the children write their names and draw a picture of what they do best on the back (blue side) of the paper. Punch a hole at the top of the snowflake and add a piece of yarn for hanging.

🍎 Hang the snowflakes on the bulletin board so the children can turn them over.

We
Are
God's
Unique
Creation

Nicholas

Lauren

Becka

Todd

Can You Match the Mittens?

*Visual discrimination   *Matching

Securely fasten two strings running parallel across the bulletin board about 10" apart. Add the title at the top.

Cut two 5" × 7" pieces of white paper per child.

Cut out two identical mitten shapes. Using crayons, markers, or paint, create identical patterns on each mitten making a matching pair.

Hang the mittens in random order on the strings with a snap clothespin. Another option is to store the mittens in a large, clear plastic bag stapled to the bulletin board.

Find the matching pairs and hang them up together.

CAN YOU MATCH THE MITTENS ?

Which Book Is Frosty's Favorite?

*Book review   *Public speaking

Cover the bulletin board with blue paper. Add polyester fluff (the kind that comes in rolls) to the bottom half to resemble snow. Add the title.

Cut three circles (small, medium, large) out of white paper for a snowman. Cut a top hat out of black paper. Cut a scarf shape out of any color paper you choose.

After you have finished reading a book, write the names of the characters in white crayon on the hat. Draw a snowman's face on the smallest white circle. Write about the setting of the book on the medium circle. Write a summary of the book, or write about the plot, on the largest circle. Write the title of the book on the scarf. Glue all the parts together to make a snowman.

Share your snowman, title, characters, setting, and plot with the class.

Add the snowmen to the bulletin board after they have been shared in class.

Help Us Decorate

*Multiplication practice

Create wreaths with corresponding berries and bows for each multiple you are studying. Laminate the pieces.

Practice by hanging each multiple and saying the equation ($7 \times 2 = 14$, and $7 \times 5 = 35$.)

A Different Twist

1. Put the answer on the back of each berry to make the activity self-correcting.
2. Allow the children to time themselves or a partner.
3. For a challenge, combine the berries from two different numbers and play two wreaths at once.

A Savior—God Keeps His Promise!

*Working with others   *Color study

Place baby Jesus in a manger in the bottom right-hand corner of the bulletin board. Glue hay or yellow Easter grass to the manger.

Cut six strips of white paper, either straight or curved. Divide the class into six groups, and assign each group a color of the rainbow.

Use magazine or wallpaper books to cut out pieces of your assigned color. Glue the pieces onto the strip until it is covered.

Staple the finished strips next to each other in proper order to create a rainbow.

A Different Twist

1. Older children can use a mixture of colors such as yellow and blue, to create green.

2. Cover the strips of white paper with colored tissue paper. Glue squares flat or wrap around the end of a pencil so they stick up.

A Savior—
GOD KEEPS HIS PROMISE!

Red
Orange
Yellow
Green
Blue
Violet

God's Family Tree

*Ordering people and events   *Old Testament history

🍎 Cover the bulletin board with background paper. Make a Christmas tree to place on the board. Add a yellow star at the top and baby Jesus at the base. Add the title to the top or side of the bulletin board. Staple nine clear plastic bags on the tree: one on baby Jesus, two side-by-side above Jesus, and six above each other leading to the star at the top of the tree.

🍎 Write one of each of these names on nine index cards: Jesus, Mary, Joseph, David, Jesse, Judah, Jacob, Isaac, and Abraham.

☺ Place the name cards in the correct bag showing the family lineage of Jesus.

💡 **A Different Twist**

1. Draw a picture of an important event in the life of each character on another index card. This is a good review of Old Testament history.

2. Put the picture cards in the bags, and match the correct name card.

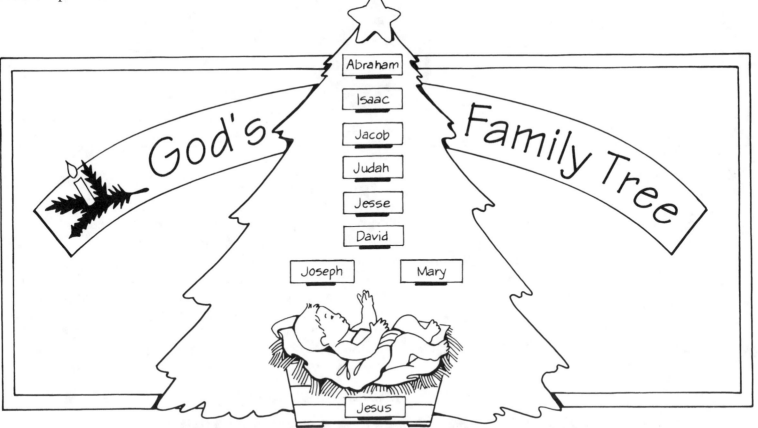

God's Family Tree

Abraham
Isaac
Jacob
Judah
Jesse
David
Joseph   Mary
Jesus

25

Guess Who's Coming
*Social studies   *Advent

Gather general information of interest to your class about school personnel (janitor, music teacher, cook, principal, etc.) Choose one mystery person every 3–4 days. Each day, add a clue to the door on the bulletin board.

Assist the children in critical thinking to determine the mystery person.

Reveal each mystery person by opening the door and showing their name or picture. Display the name or picture on the board and pray for that person.

During the last week of Advent, put Jesus behind the door. Build anticipation of His coming with facts—He was baptized by His cousin; He healed the sick; He used to be a carpenter—as well as anything you have been studying about Jesus.

 A Different Twist

1. Have each mystery person actually come through your classroom door to reveal their identity.
2. Ask the mystery people for specific prayer requests.
3. Allow the children to seek out and prepare information for the mystery persons.

GUESS
WHO'S
COMING

?

Blue
eyes

sings
well

Mr. W

dog
Holly

likes
pizza

goes
fishing

Name That Tune!

*Learning Christmas hymns

 Designate which hymns you will include in this game by writing the title and number on one of the hymnals you have placed on the bulletin board.

 Prepare blank strips of paper that will fit on the open hymnals on the board. Place the strips near the board. Attach a large envelope to the board to hold completed strips.

On blank strips of paper, write the lines of one of the designated hymns. Put these inside the envelope for someone else to choose.

Choose a strip of paper out of the envelope. Read it and decide which hymn it belongs to. Place it on the correct hymnal on the board.

Designate new hymns each week.

A Different Twist

1. Set a timer and allow the children to time themselves or each other.
2. Place all the lines to one verse of each familiar hymn in the envelope. Have the children put them in order to build entire verses.

Our Birthday Gifts for Jesus

*Fine motor skills   *Identifying gifts and talents

🍎 Cover the bulletin board with light-colored paper, and add the title.

🙂 Place one of your hands on green paper. Trace your open hand. Cut out your green hand shape.

🍎 Place the green hand shapes on the bulletin board, fingers down, to create the shape of a Christmas tree. Start with six or seven on the bottom and work your way up.

🍎 Copy two gift box patterns per child (see pattern on page 58).

🍎 Share with the children that God gave the greatest gift to us when He sent His Son, Jesus, to be our Savior. Discuss the kinds of gifts we can give as an offering back to our Lord: voice to sing praises, helping others, visiting a shut-in, etc.

🙂 Cut out both gift boxes, and staple them together at the top.

🙂 Decorate the outside gift box, and write your name on the tag.

🙂 Use the inside gift box to draw or write about the gift you would like to give to Jesus.

💡 A Different Twist

1. Use wallpaper samples or Christmas gift wrap for the outside gift box and white paper for the inside box.

⭐ Our Birthday Gifts for Jesus ⭐

The Twelve Days of Christmas

*Grouping by attributes   *Problem solving

☺ Work in pairs to illustrate one of the twelve gifts in the song "The Twelve Days of Christmas." Draw your picture on a piece of 9" × 12" construction paper. Each pair should do a different gift.

🍎 Hang the pictures of the twelve gifts along the bottom of the bulletin board. Add the title. Attach a bag on the side of the bulletin board for strips of blank paper that can be used for labeling.

☺ Group the twelve gifts according to attributes such as people, animals, musical instruments, etc. Be creative. Use blank strips of paper to give the group a title, and pin the papers by the group.

What Does Immanuel Mean? God with Us

*Writing and drawing   *Study of Jesus' life

Discuss the meaning of the name "Immanuel" (see Matthew 1:23). Jesus was true God and true man dwelling on earth. What a gift!

Use a 9" × 12" piece of white paper to draw a picture of a favorite Bible story about Jesus. Write why this is your favorite story. Tell how Jesus showed that He was both God and man.

Add ribbon and a bow so your picture looks like a gift.

Staple the gifts to the bulletin board.

What Does Immanuel Mean?

God with Us

A New Year

*Setting goals   *Corporate prayer   *Writing skills

Use a variety of colors to make copies of a balloon and party hat for each chid (see pattern on page 59).

Write and/or draw a picture about a favorite memory from the past year on the balloon shape. Write and/or draw a goal for the new year on the hat shape.

Take turns praying that the Lord will help you and your friends reach your goals.

Staple the balloons and hats on the bulletin board. Add curling ribbon to give the board a festive appearance.

A New Year

What Will the Next Century Be Like?

*Social studies   *Compare and contrast

Divide the board down the middle. Place a large paper arrow across the top of the board. Staple the title on the arrow. Label the left side as "The 20th Century" and the right as "The 21st Century."

Collect a variety of magazines featuring pictures of people and current events.

Cut pictures out of the magazines that show things that represent the 20th Century. Work in groups to include topics such as homes, transportation, occupations, and clothing.

Draw a picture of what you think might happen in the 21st Century. Include some of the topics listed above.

Add the pictures to the proper sides of the board.

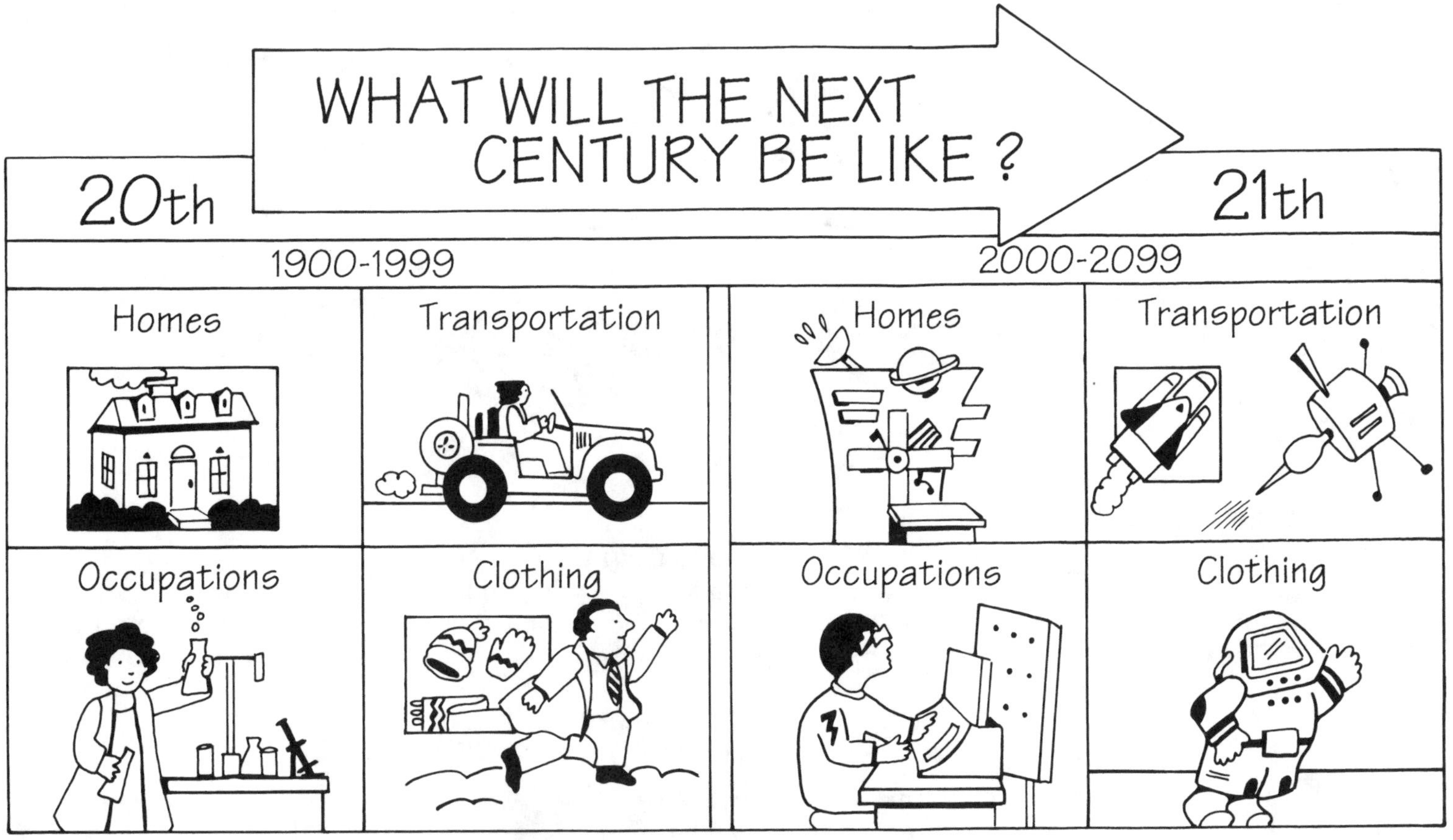

WHAT WILL THE NEXT CENTURY BE LIKE ?

20th		21th	
1900-1999		2000-2099	
Homes	Transportation	Homes	Transportation
Occupations	Clothing	Occupations	Clothing

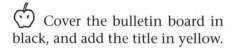 # Celebrate Epiphany—Jesus Is Our Guiding Light
*Bible study   *Understanding the church year   *Working in groups

Cover the bulletin board in black, and add the title in yellow.

Place a large, yellow paper candle and flame in the center of the board. Place the letters J-E-S-U-S on the candle. Staple candle so that it curves outward to give it dimension. Use tissue paper or cellophane for the flame.

Cut several 3" × 12" strips of yellow paper.

Work with a partner, and look up Bible verses that give various names for Jesus. Write these names on the strips of yellow paper. Find as many different names as possible.

Discuss what each name means and what it tells us about the character of Jesus. Staple the strips around the candle.

Epiphany—Jesus Came to Save All

*Fine motor skills *Creativity

Cut the title out of yellow or white paper. Cut an 8" × 10" piece of yellow paper for each child. Gather items for embellishment such as glitter, sequins, and gold or silver curling ribbon.

Use a piece of yellow paper to design a star. Write your name in the center of the star and decorate it.

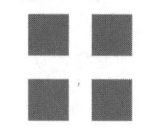

A Different Twist

1. Glue a small picture of the child in the center of the star.

What Are You Doing, Mr. Groundhog?

*Creative thinking   *Graphing

Cover the top half of the bulletin board with blue paper and the bottom half with brown.

Draw underground trails and dens on the brown paper, creating one den for each child.

Cut one circle out of brown paper and one circle out of white paper.

On the white circle, draw a picture of something the groundhog is doing. On the brown circle, write your name.

Glue your white circle in one of the dens on the brown paper. Staple the brown circle over the den to make a cover that can be lifted.

Create a graph where children can vote whether or not Mr. Groundhog saw his shadow. Place the graph on the top half of the board.

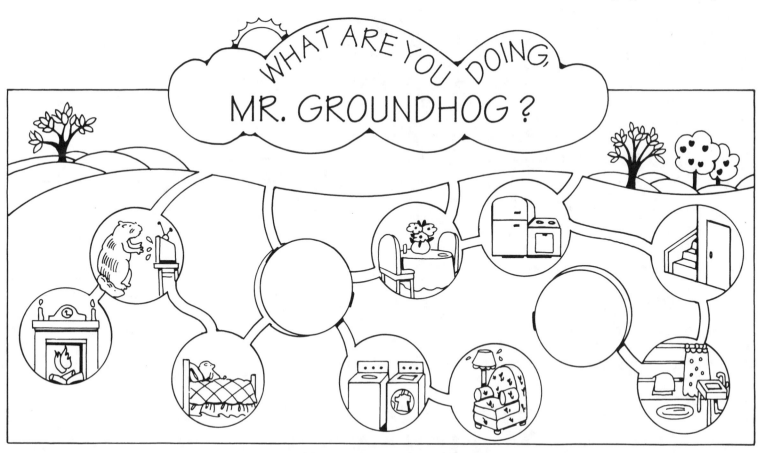

WHAT ARE YOU DOING, MR. GROUNDHOG?

God Is Love

*Fine motor skills   *Bible study skills

☺ Cut a heart out of pink or white paper. Use red paper or a doily to cut out a larger heart. Glue the smaller heart on top of the larger one.

🍎 Divide children into small groups or pairs.

☺ Find a favorite Bible verse about God's love, and write the verse on your heart.

🍎 Collect the hearts, and arrange them into the shape of a cross on the bulletin board. Add the title.

God Is Love

You Are Loved

*Using descriptive language   *Encouraging others

Measure and cut white background paper.

Decorate the white background with hearts, using a variety of mediums.

Cut two hearts out of pink or red paper. Draw or glue a picture of yourself on one of the hearts. (A real photo is more exciting.) Finish the sentence, "God made me special because …" on the second heart.

Have the children share two things they like or enjoy about each child. Encourage descriptive language.

Write what was shared about you on your second heart. Staple the hearts together with your picture-heart underneath.

Add everyone's heart to the bulletin board.

Look at what is written on each heart, and try to guess whose picture is underneath.

37

God Loves Me ... I Love You!
*Opposites *The Ten Commandments

Assign one commandment to each child or group of children. Distribute large hearts cut out of heavy paper.

Cut the heart in half as for a puzzle. On one half of the heart, write or illustrate what we should NOT do according to the commandment. On the other half, write or illustrate what we SHOULD do according to the commandment. On the back of each half, write the number of the commandment.

Review the commandments by matching the mixed-up hearts. Try to recite each commandment as you play.

God Loves Me ...I Love You

I   II   III   IV   V   VI   VII   VIII   IX   X

A Different Twist

1. Use as a language arts game to learn opposites.
2. Have the children work in pairs. Give each pair a large heart and two opposite words.
3. Cut the heart in half, and write and illustrate each word. Play the game by matching the mixed-up hearts.

38

How Well Do You Know These Presidents?

*Reviewing historical facts

Divide the bulletin board in half. Place a picture of President Washington on one side and President Lincoln on the other. Staple two plastic bags at the bottom. Place push pins in one bag.

Gather reference books, such as encyclopedias and biography books. Or use the Internet, if available. This could be a homework assignment also.

Work in small groups. Do research to discover three facts about each president. Use the various references provided. Write these facts on three index cards. Share the facts with the whole class.

Place the index cards in the other bag at the bottom of the board. Prepare an answer key the children can use for self-checking.

Work alone or in pairs to place the fact cards by the correct president. Self-check using the key provided.

Meet the Saints

*All Saints' Day/History

Make a crown, representing their heavenly crown, for each child.

Write a short report on a saint who has gone to heaven. This can be a Bible character, church father, relative, etc. Make a cutout picture of that person wearing a crown.

Provide verses, such as 1 Peter 2:9, 1 John 3:1, Ephesians 2:19–22, 2 Corinthians 5:17, to help children describe themselves as saints.

Write a similar report and make a cutout of yourself.

Add the crowns to the children's cutouts of themselves. Have the children share their thoughts about going to heaven.

 **A Different Twist**

1. Allow the children to decorate the upper section of the background to show how they picture heaven.

2. Allow children to add their own decorations to the crowns they make.

Meet the Saints

What's in a Friendship?
*Building friendships

☺ Write a characteristic of a good friendship on a recipe card. Make it sound like an ingredient that could be used in a recipe for friendship (i.e., "2 cups of listening").

🍎 Collect the cards.

🍎 As you note "friendly" behavior being displayed, give the children appropriate cards with friendship ingredients listed. They need not receive their own cards to hang.

☺ Hang the cards on the bulletin board as you get them, or at a designated time during the day.

WHAT'S IN A FRIENDSHIP ?

"A friend loves at all times." Prov. 17:17

2 cups listening

1 tsp. smiles

3 Tbs. love

1 cup hugs

💡 A Different Twist

1. In addition to recipe cards, place pictures of things that strengthen a friendship "in the pot"—Bibles, crosses, churches, toys or games, smiles. These could be made by the children or cut from magazines.

2. Before taking down the bulletin board, allow each child to write his or her own complete recipe for friendship as a creative writing assignment. Remove the recipe cards and hang the creative writing assignments on the pot.

3. Add photographs of the children to the pot. Be sure to include a picture of Jesus, our best Friend.

What Kind of Pie Am I?

*Fractions

Provide various sizes of circles for each child to use to make their pies.

Color and decorate your favorite kind of pie(s). Cut them out.

Collect the pies.

Use a black marker to clearly draw lines on each child's pie, dividing them into the various fractional amounts you wish to study (fourths, tenths, halves, etc.)

Make corresponding labels for each section of the bulletin board (fourths, tenths, halves, etc.)

Punch a hole in the top of each pie. Place push pins at various places on the bulletin board so the children can hang their pies.

Hang your pies in the appropriate sections.

What Kind of Pie Am I ?

| halves | thirds | fourths | eighths |

A Different Twist

1. Periodically rearrange the sections of the bulletin board.
2. Include some pies obviously divided into unequal fractional parts. Have a "reject" or "nonfractional" section.

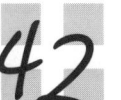

You're Packed!

*Remembering Baptism   *Life as God's child

When attaching the baptismal font to the bulletin board, leave the top open so items may be tucked behind it.

Cut out pictures that symbolize the following (or, just write these words on individual cards): hymnal, Bible, communion, prayer, pastor, church, other Christians (a string of paper dolls would work well) Sunday school, teachers, home, and Christian books. Place these pictures in the font on the bulletin board.

Talk about Baptism. Visit the sanctuary to see the baptismal font.

Choose one child each day during devotions to reach into the font and pull out a picture. Allow another child to staple the picture onto the backpack. Discuss how children pack their backpacks to be prepared for school. Draw a connection to the fact that, in Baptism, God supplies us, as His children, with all we need to live and grow in Him.

A Different Twist

1. Have the children make shapes or words for each other. Give each one a "personal backpack" to tape inside their desk lid as a reminder of the blessings that are part of being God's child.

How great is the love the Father has lavished on us, that we should be called children of God.

1 John 3:1

You're Packed!

God Made Us Alike—and Different

*Diagraming   *Self-awareness

Obtain a photo of everyone in your class, including yourself.

Label the three portions of your Venn diagram. Use these or other ideas:

- walks to school/walks or rides/rides
- likes ketchup on hotdogs/likes ketchup and mustard/likes mustard
- likes math/likes math and reading/likes reading
- likes lunch/likes recess and lunch/likes recess
- has brothers/has brothers and sisters/has sisters
- likes winter/likes winter and summer/likes summer
- God's child/God's child and going to heaven/going to heaven (place everyone in the middle, this time!)

Place your photo in the correct place in the diagram.

Relabel the three parts of the diagram each week and play again.

💡 A Different Twist

1. Make the diagram more complex by using three or more circles.

God Made Us Alike—and Different

walks

rides

walks or rides

44

Have No Fear!
*Using God's Word

Set out various resources that would help the children locate Bible truths. Bibles, Bible story books, concordances, and references of past memory verses work well.

Cut out lots of crows and lots of "happy people" shapes (see pattern on page 60). Place these in an accessible place near the board.

Write something you are afraid of on one of the crows. Don't include your name. Staple the crow to the bulletin board.

Read about someone's fear. Find a Bible verse to help that person handle their fear. Write the Bible verse on a happy face, and staple it near the crow.

Discuss how fears are real; they will still be there, just like the crows, but God, through His Word, helps His children face their fears.

A Different Twist

1. If looking up verses is too difficult, allow the children to use words of encouragement regarding God's love and Bible truths they have learned.

In These Last Days ... He Has Spoken to Us through His Son

*End Times   *Promises of Jesus

Set out red-letter editions of the Bible so the words of Jesus are easy to find. Put bookmarks in each of the four Gospels. Set out two different kinds of paper—bright, happy colors for heaven, and blue or green for the earth.

Write a Bible verse on the rainbow, such as John 14:6, that tells that Jesus is the way to heaven. Or add a picture of Jesus or a cross to the rainbow.

Look for the words of Jesus that are written in red letters. Find verses that tell about His promises. If you read a promise about God's care on earth, write it on a piece of paper and add it to the earth collage. If you find a promise about heaven, add it to the heaven collage, using appropriate colors.

"No one comes to the Father except through Me."
John 14:6

IN THESE LAST DAYS...
HE HAS SPOKEN TO US THROUGH
HIS SON

💡 A Different Twist

1. Have someone read the verses to children who can't read. Have them add the appropriate piece of colored paper to the collage.

How Wide Is Clyde?

*Measuring/Estimating

🍎 Cut sections of Clyde's sweater, each a different size, for each child.

☺ Decorate your section of Clyde's sweater.

☺ Play this game with a partner. One partner should build Clyde's sweater and attach his tail. Have the other partner estimate the length of the sweater, and then measure the actual length.

☺ Store the sweaters in "Clyde's closet."

💡 **A Different Twist**

1. Make sweaters from old wallpaper samples or heavy fabric swatches.

2. Use different units for measuring, even unusual ones, such as pencils, math books, etc.

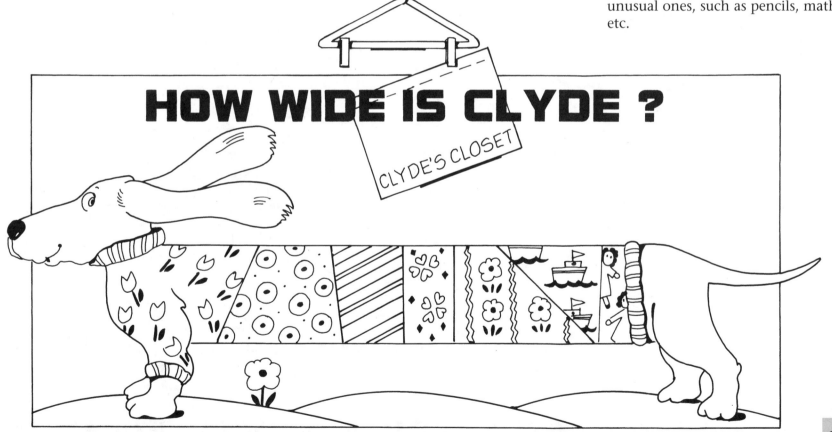

HOW WIDE IS CLYDE ?

CLYDE'S CLOSET

What Kind of Tracks Do You Leave?

*Witnessing   *Visual discrimination

☺ Trace around your shoes and cut the shoe out. Design the shoes as footprints that show gifts you might use to witness and share your faith with others you meet. Or tell what types of encouragement you like to use to share the love of Jesus with others.

WHAT KIND OF TRACKS DO YOU LEAVE ?

1. Allow younger children to play a game by removing the tracks and hanging them up again in pairs.
2. For older children, display all the pairs of prints. Each day, remove one set of prints and see if the children can recall which pair is missing. Talk about how much that person is missed when he or she is absent.

Get to Know U.S.!

*Geography

🍎 Cut rectangles for each state out of poster board. Assign states to children or groups of children.

😊 Cut the rectangle vertically to create two puzzle pieces. On the left side, draw the state and label it. On the right side, draw pictures of products or services given to us by that state or something for which the state is famous.

😊 Mix up the pieces and play a matching game.

🍎 You may wish to have two sets of puzzles with only 25 states in each set.

💡 **A Different Twist**

1. Hang a United States map nearby for reference.

2. Make new right halves for each state, containing other information (i.e. the capital city or the state's population), or create more than two puzzle pieces, containing all the facts.

3. Make two-piece puzzles to learn shapes and names for states that have an obvious shape.

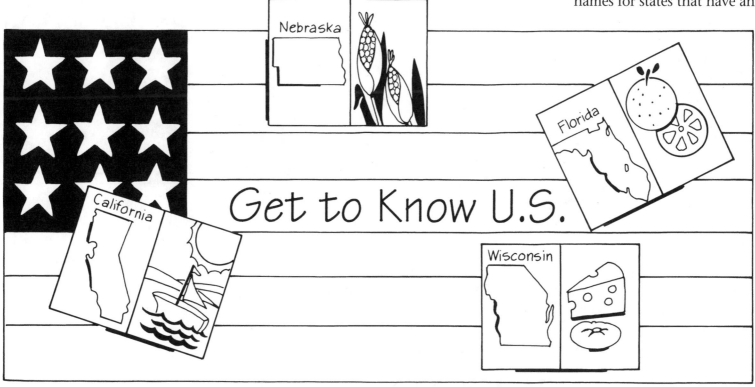

Nebraska

Florida

California

Get to Know U.S.

Wisconsin

What Do You See?
*Science/Constellations

☺ Make several stars of different shapes and sizes.

☺ To play, build a well-known constellation or make up your own.

🍎 Help the children name their original constellations.

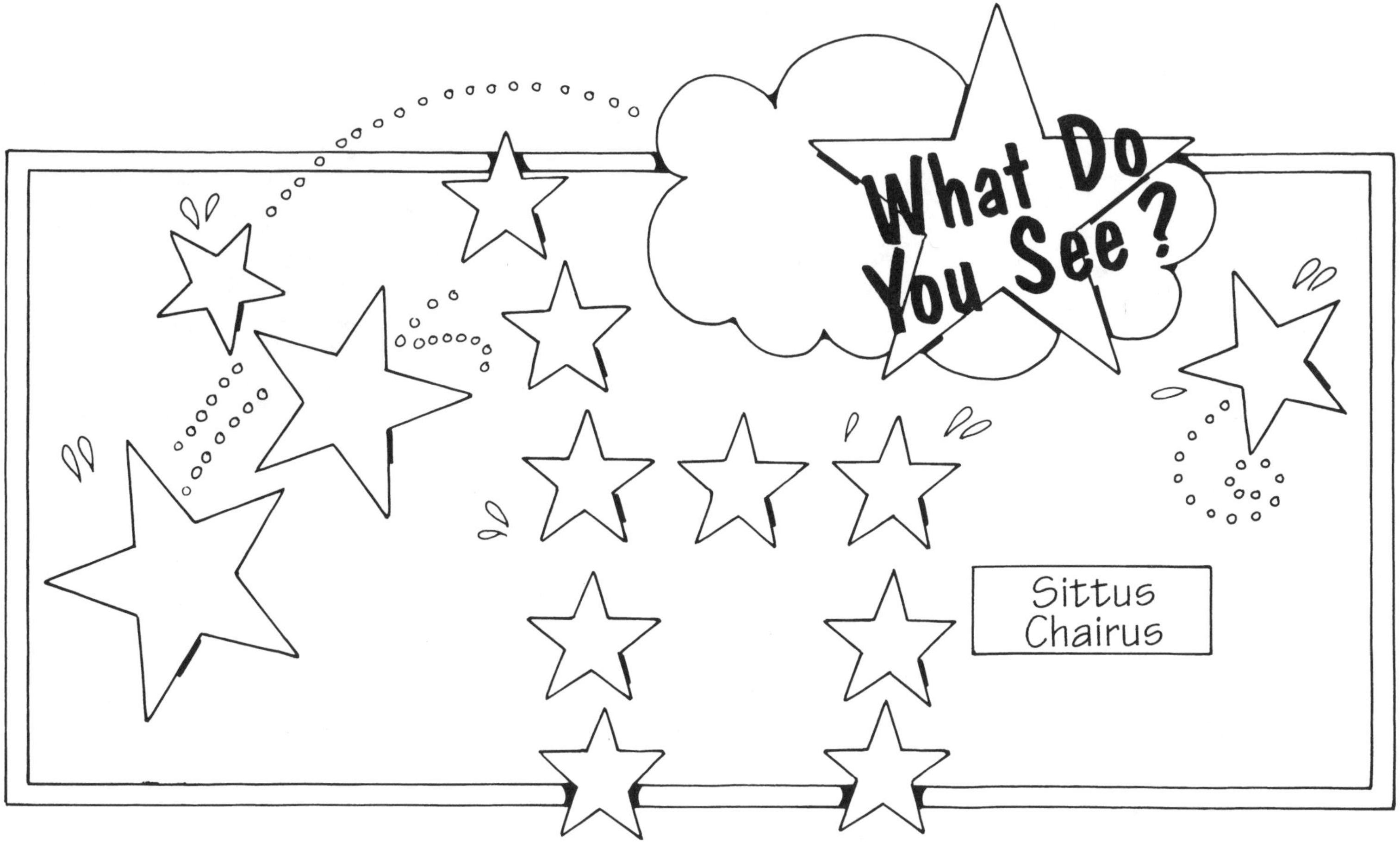

What Do You See?

Sittus Chairus

 A Different Twist

1. Research how some of our constellations got their names.
2. Create a constellation for the class. Allow the children to decipher what they see, name the constellation, and write a story about how it got its name.

For God So Loved the World ...

*Missions   *Geography

☺ Choose a country and make a star showing that Jesus came as Savior for everyone living in that country. Decorate the star. Attach it with a clothespin to the bulletin board.

☺ Tie a piece of yarn to each clothespin. Put a push pin in each country on the map.

☺ Pull each yarn over to the correct push pin to show the location of each country.

For God So Loved the World...

Argentina Chile France Haiti Nigeria Togo Wales

💡 A Different Twist

1. Obtain information about missionaries in some of the areas. Pray for them and/or write to them.
2. For a challenge, have the children hang the countries in alphabetical order.
3. Make cardboard stars and cover them with foil, writing the names with puff paints.
4. Obtain information about the number of Christians and/or unchurched people in each country. Add these numbers to the stars, and then have children hang them in numerical order.

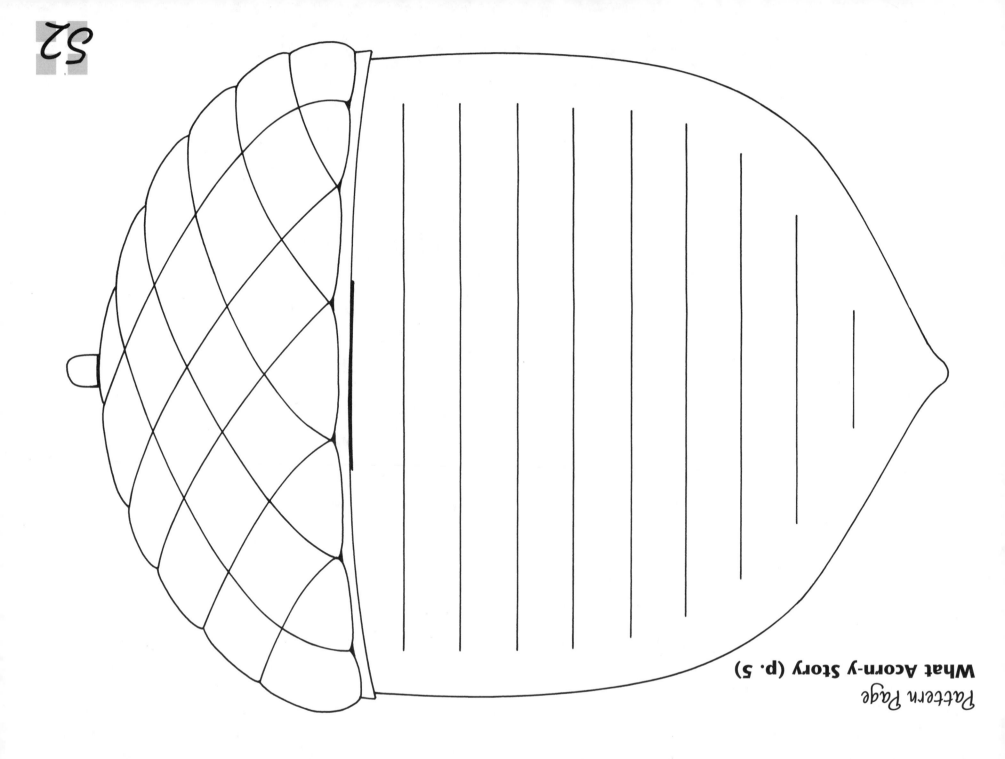

Pattern Page
What Acorn-y Story (p. 5)

Pattern Page
Piles of Practice (p. 6)

53

54

How Can Jesus' Light Shine through Me? (p. 9)

Pattern Page

Pattern Page
Faith Alone, Grace Alone, Scripture Alone (p. 10)

55

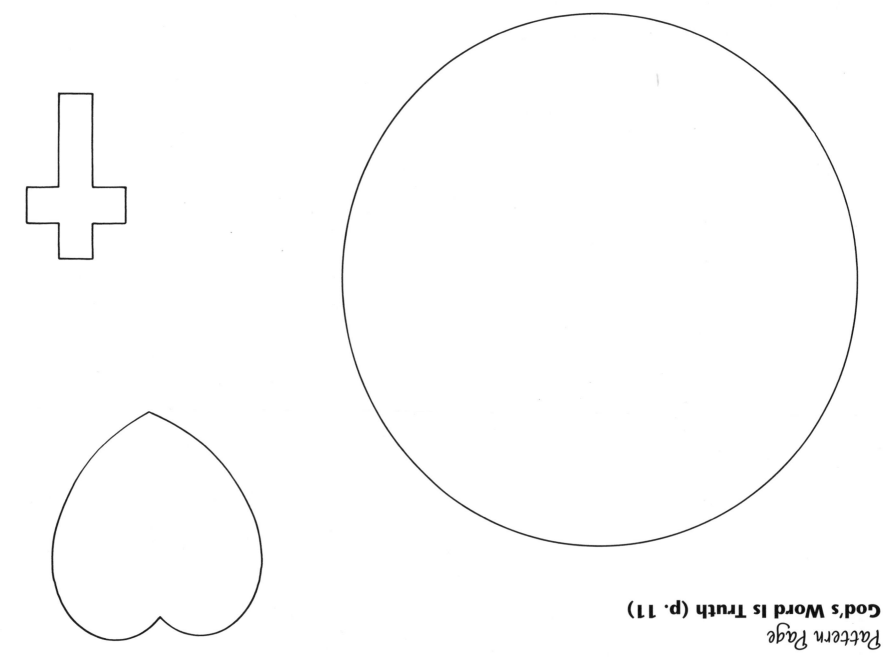

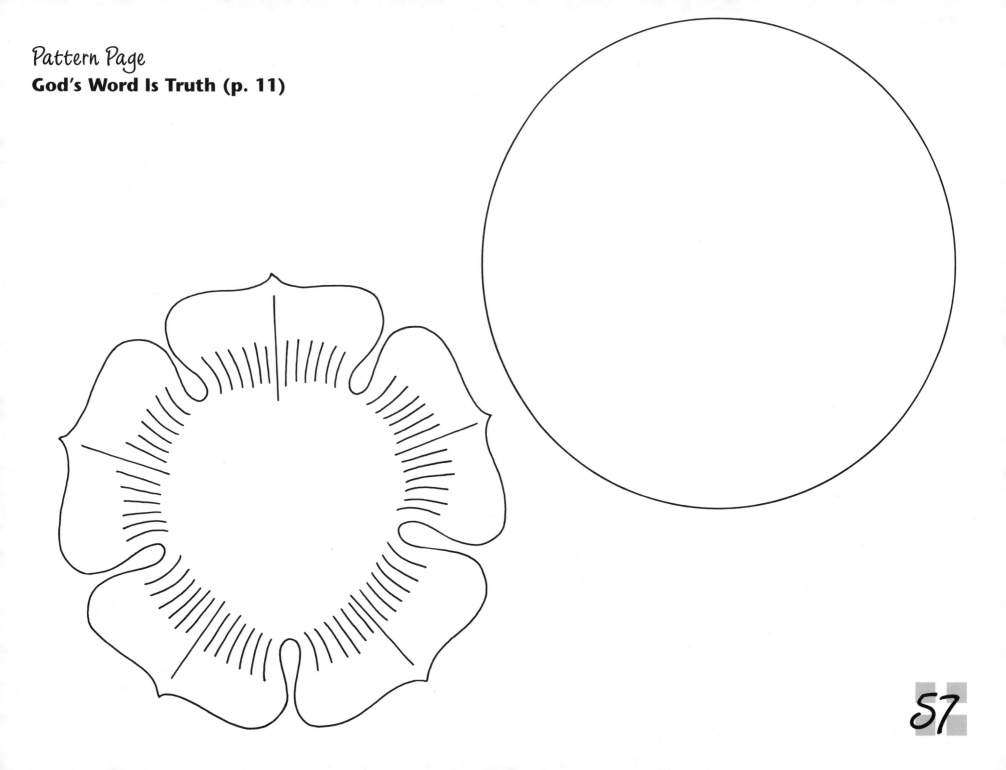

57

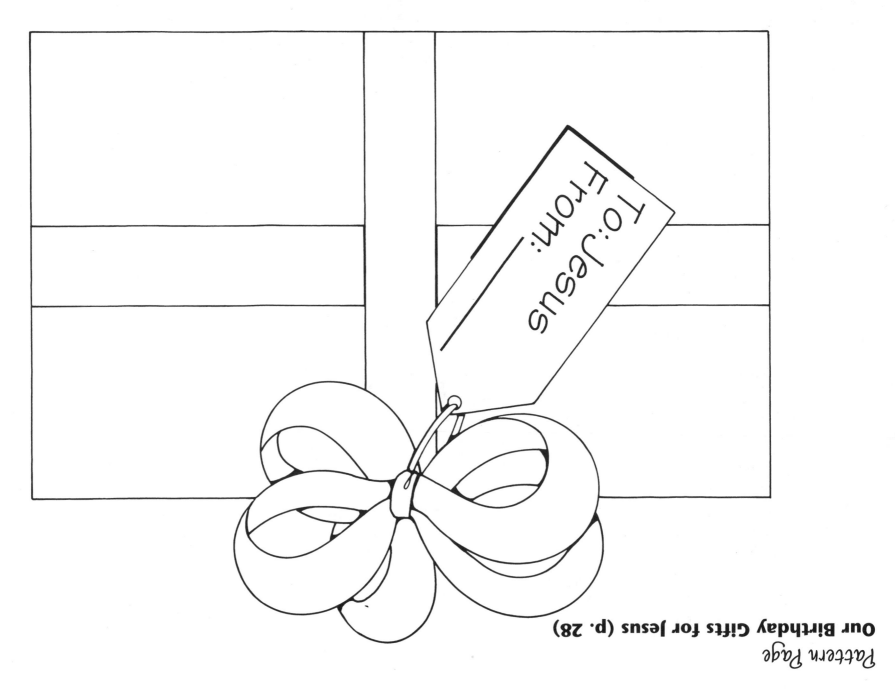

To: Jesus

From: _____

Pattern Page
Our Birthday Gifts for Jesus (p. 28)

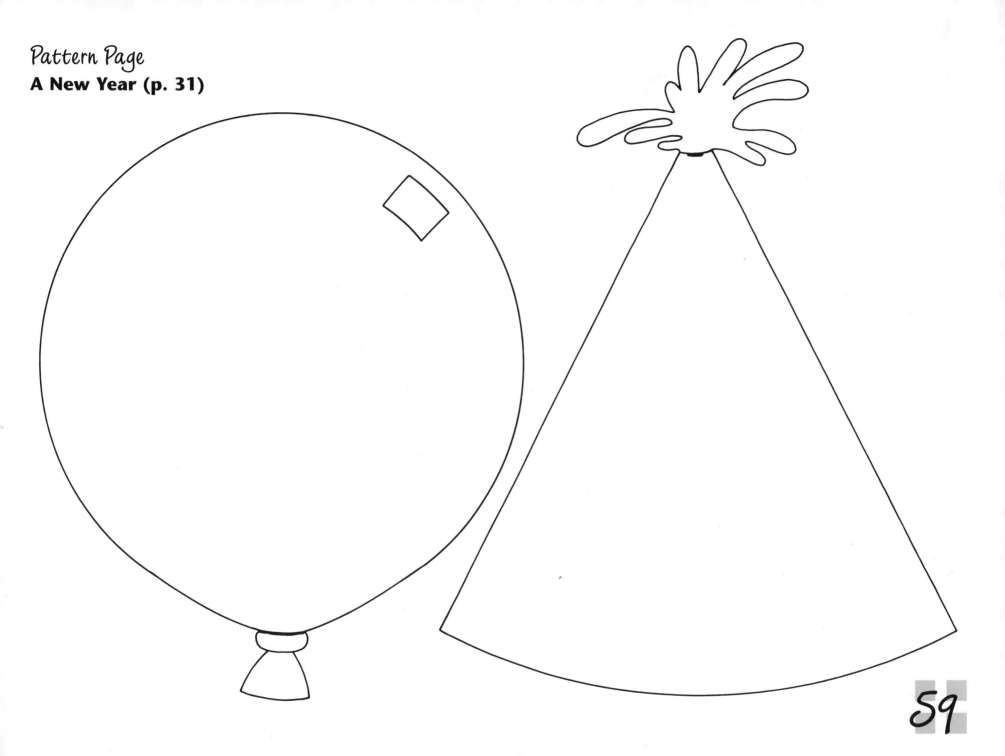